Contents

KT-116-182

I am a big boy now ...

... but once I was
a little baby.

When I
was a baby,
my mum
fed me.

I played
on my
play mat.

I had to wear
a nappy.

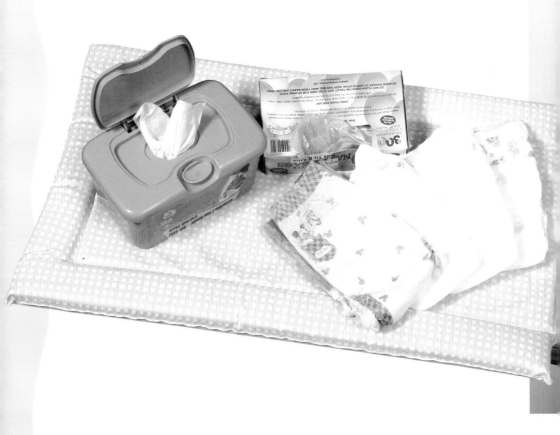

I made baby noises.

When I was a toddler, I sat in a high chair.

14

15

16

I had to use a potty.

18

I pushed my baby walker.

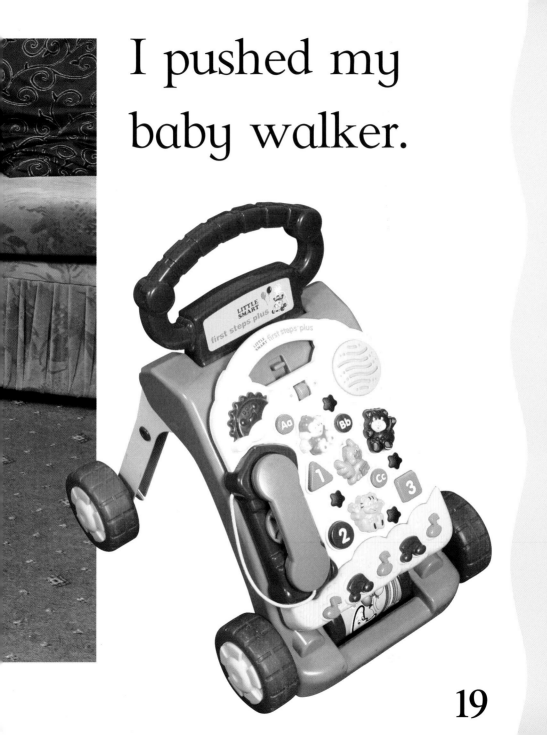

I learned lots of words.

Mama

21

22

I'm glad I'm a big boy now.

Word bank

Look back for these words and pictures.

Baby

Baby walker

Boy

High chair

Juice

Nappy

Play mat

Potty

Toddler